Life Flows on the River of Love

by

Blythe Ayne

Life Flows on the River of Love

by

Blythe Ayne

Life Flows on the River of Love
Blythe Ayne

Emerson & Tilman, Publishers
129 Pendleton Way #55
Washougal, WA 98671

www.LifeFlowsOnTheRiverOfLove.BlytheAyne.com
www.HornOfPlenty.BlytheAyne.com

All Rights Reserved
No part of this publication may be reproduced, distributed, or transmitted
in any form, or by any means, including photocopying, recording,
or other electronic or mechanical methods, without the prior
written permission of the author, except brief quotations
in critical reviews and other noncommercial
uses permitted by copyright law.

Book & cover design by Blythe Ayne
All Text & Graphics © 2017 Blythe Ayne

Life Flows on the River of Love

www.BlytheAyne.com

The text herein is from my other works, including: *Horn of Plenty, Our Walk, The Light of Your Heart, A Perfect Life, The Path, Love Yourself, An Angel's Visit, The Listening Universe,* and my *Nature Guidance* card deck & book, and others. These works may also be found on *Instagram, Pintarest, Google +, Facebook, Twitter,* and other internet sites as well as my website: www.BlytheAyne.com

Life Flows on the River of Love
is available on Gumroad and Amazon as an ebook and physical book
ISBN13: 978-0-9827835-9-7

[1. BODY, MIND & SPIRIT / Inspiration
2. BODY, MIND & SPIRIT / Mindfulness & Meditation
3. POETRY / General] I. Title.
BIC: FM

First Edition

YOUR HEART KNOWS THE WAY

© Blythe Ayne

In Cat's Eyes

In my eye reflects
Everything you do
Think about your actions
And to your Cat be true

If you believe Cat just sits
Staring, mute and unaware
I advise you to think twice
When you see that far away stare

'Cause Cat tracks everything
Cat knows what's in your mind
Cat sees your every action
If you're mean, and when you're kind

Did you ever wonder
Why Cat is everywhere?
It's for the record, Human
So, be thoughtful and beware!

Let the record show
You were always loving and kind
'Cause Cat knows actions reflect
What is on your mind!

©Blythe Ayne

Heart-Mind In Balance

From: Horn of Plenty © Blythe Ayne

Image & Text © Blythe Ayne

Every dream you ever dreamed is right here in your pocket

© Blythe Ayne

Your splendor is astounding
From Source you become more than was there
An alchemy of the Cosmos
Precious, dazzling, and rare.

©Blythe Ayne

Whatever you desire
Affirm that it's on its way

Then release the thought

from: Horn of Plenty ©Blythe Ayne

Believe me when I say, my Friend,
In your every breath Angels abide,
They lean over you with Love and Care,
They are always by your side.

You have nothing to lose to call, "Angels!"
Whenever life's woes get you down,
Your Angels will rush to attend you,
For in spirit you wear a crown.

Winter's Crown

Holly, crown of winter
Powerful, life-protecting tree
Brings good fortune to the home
And warm vitality

Holly in the yard stands guard
Only lets kind spirits here
Cross my threshold and you'll find
My holly home is filled with cheer.

©Blythe Ayne

Books & Audio by Blythe Ayne

Fiction:
The Darling Undesirables Series:
The Heart of Leo - short story prequel
The Darling Undesirables
www.TheDarlingUndesirables.BlytheAyne.com
Moons Rising
www.MoonsRising.BlytheAyne.com
The Inventor's Clone
www.TheInventorsClone.BlytheAyne.com
Hearts Quest
www.HeartsQuest.BlytheAyne.com

Short Story Collections:
5 Minute Stories
Lovely Frights for Lonely Nights

Children's Illustrated Books:
The Rat Who Didn't Like Rats
The Rat Who Didn't Like Christmas

Nonfiction:
Love Is The Answer
45 Ways To Excellent Life
Horn of Plenty — The Cornucopia of Your Life
Save Your Life Series:
Save Your Life With The Power Of pH Balance
Save Your Life With The Phenomenal Lemon
Save Your Life with Stupendous Spices

Poetry:
Home & the Surrounding Territory

CD:
The Power of pH Balance –
Dr. Blythe Ayne Interviews Steven Acuff

About the Author

Blythe Ayne lives on ten acres of forest in the Pacific NW with a few domestic and numerous wild creatures, where she creates an ever-growing inventory of books. Her articles, short stories and poetry have appeared in hundreds of publications.

An insatiable student of the human condition, she has a Ph.D. in Social Psychology and Ethnography from the University of California, Irvine.

Visit www.BlytheAyne.com for more information about Blythe's books, art, and appearances.

www.ingramcontent.com/pod-product-compliance
Lightning Source LLC
Chambersburg PA
CBHW061123010526
44112CB00025B/2954